Falling Water

Also by John Koethe

POETRY

> *Blue Vents*
> *Domes*
> *The Late Wisconsin Spring*

PHILOSOPHY

> *The Continuity of Wittgenstein's Thought*

Falling Water

poems by
JOHN KOETHE

HarperPerennial
A Division of HarperCollinsPublishers

The poems in this book have been published in the following magazines:

The American Poetry Review: "The Constant Voice," "Henrietta," "Morning in America"

Bellingham Review: "The Interior of the Future"

Boulevard: "The Realm of Ends"

Grand Street: "The Third Wish"

Gulf Coast: "Sorrento Valley"

The New Republic: "Friends," "From the Porch"

Southwest Review: "Argument in Isolation," "A Pathetic Landscape," "The Secret Amplitude"

TriQuarterly: "Early Morning in Milwaukee"

Western Humanities Review: "Falling Water"

The Yale Review: "Songs My Mother Taught Me"

"Morning in America" was reprinted in *The Best American Poetry 1991*, Mark Strand and David Lehman, eds.; and "Falling Water" in *The Best American Poetry 1995*, Richard Howard and David Lehman, eds. (both published by Scribner's).

HarperCollins books may be purchased for educational, business, or sales promotional use. For information please write: Special Markets Department, HarperCollins Publishers, Inc., 10 East 53rd Street, New York, NY 10022.

FIRST EDITION

Designed by Elina D. Nudelman

Library of Congress Cataloging-in-Publication Data

Koethe, John, 1945–

    Falling water : poems / John Koethe. — 1st ed.
      p. cm.
    ISBN 0–06–055371–5 (hardcover). —ISBN 0–06–095257–1 (pbk.)
    I. Title.
  PS3561.O35F3 1997 APR 13 '99
  811'.54—dc21   97-4254

97 98 99 00 01 ❖/RRD 10 9 8 7 6 5 4 3 2 1

  98 99 00 01 ❖/RRD 10 9 8 7 6 5 4 3 2 (pbk.)

For Mary Kinzie

I am grateful to the editors of Southwest Review *for awarding the 1989 Elizabeth Machette Stover Award to "A Pathetic Landscape"; and to the John Simon Guggenheim Memorial Foundation, the Milwaukee Arts Foundation, and the National Endowment for the Arts for fellowships which were of great help in writing many of these poems.*

Contents

From the Porch

The stores were bright, and not too far from home.
The school was only half a mile from downtown,
A few blocks from the Oldsmobile dealer. In the sky,
The airplanes came in low towards Lindbergh Field,
Passing overhead with a roar that shook the windows.
How *inert* the earth must look from far away:
The morning mail, the fantasies, the individual days
Too intimate to see, no matter how you tried;
The photos in the album of the young man leaving home.
Yet there was always time to visit them again
In a roundabout way, like the figures in the stars,
Or a life traced back to its imaginary source
In an adolescent reverie, a forgotten book—
As though one's childhood were a small midwestern town
Some forty years ago, before the elm trees died.
September was a modern classroom and the latest cars,
That made a sort of futuristic dream, circa 1955.
The earth was still uncircled. You could set your course
On the day after tomorrow. And children fell asleep
To the lullaby of people murmuring softly in the kitchen,
While a breeze rustled the pages of *Life* magazine,
And the wicker chairs stood empty on the screened-in porch.

The Constant Voice

Above a coast that lies between two coasts
Flight 902 turns west towards San Diego.
Milwaukee falls away. The constant passenger,
Removed from character and context, resumes
His California story, gradually ascending,
Reading *Farewell, My Lovely* for the umpteenth time,
Like a book above the world, or below the noise.
I recall some houses half-way in the desert,
And how dry the trees all seemed, and temporary
Even the tallest buildings looked, with bungalows
Decaying in the Santa Ana wind. And finally
Just how small it was, and mean. Is it nostalgia
For the limited that makes the days go quickly,
Tracing out their spirals of diminishing concern?
Like all the boys who lived on Westland Avenue,
I learned to follow the trails through the canyon,
Shoot at birds with a BB-gun, and dream of leaving.
What *are* books? To me they seemed like mirrors
Holding up a vision of the social, in which people,
Beckoning from their inaccessible preserves
Like forgotten toys, afforded glimpses of those
Evanescent worlds that certain minor writers
—Raymond Chandler say, or even Rupert Brooke—
Could visualize somehow, and bring to life again.
And though these worlds were sometimes difficult to see,
Once having seen them one returned to find the words
Still there, like a part of the surroundings
Compliant to one's will.

Yet these are attitudes,
And each age has its separate store of attitudes,
Its store of tropes—"In Grantchester, in Grantchester!—"
That filter through its dreams and fill its songs.
Hume tried to show that sympathy alone allows
"The happiness of strangers" to affect our lives.
Yet now and then a phrase, echoing in the mind
Long after its occasion, seems to resurrect
A world I think I recognize, and never saw.
For what was there to see? Some houses on a hill
Next to a small stream? A village filled with people
I couldn't understand? Could anyone have *seen* the
Transitory sweetness of the Georgians' England
And the world before the War, before *The Waste Land*?
Years are secrets, and their memories are often
Stories of a past that no one witnessed, like the
Fantasies of home one builds to rationalize
The ordinary way one's life has gone since then.
Words seem to crystallize that life in pictures—
In a postcard of a vicarage, or of a canyon
Wedged between the desert and an endless ocean—
But their clarity is fleeting. I can nearly
See the coast from here, and as I hear the engines
And the bell chimes, all those images dissolve.
And then I start to hear the murmur of that
Constant voice as distant from me as a landscape
Studied from an airplane: a contingent person
With a particular mind, and a particular will,
Descending across a desert, westward over mountains

And the sparsely peopled scrub beyond the city,
Pocked with half-filled reservoirs and rudimentary
Trails with nothing waiting for me at the end
—"And is there honey still for tea?"—
But isolated houses nestled in the hills.

Sorrento Valley

On a hillside somewhere in Sorrento Valley,
My aunts and uncles sat in canvas chairs
In the blazing sun, facing a small ash tree.

There was no wind. In the distance I could see
Some modern buildings, hovering in the air
Above the wooded hillsides of Sorrento Valley.

I followed the progress of a large bumblebee
As the minister stood, offering a prayer,
Next to the young white California ash tree.

Somewhere a singer went right on repeating
When I Grow Too Old to Dream. Yet to dream where,
I wondered—on a hillside in Sorrento Valley,

Half-way between the mountains and the sea?
To be invisible at last, and released from care,
Beneath a stone next to a white tree?

—As though each of us were alone, and free,
And the common ground we ultimately shared
Were on a hillside somewhere in Sorrento Valley,
In the shade of a small ash tree.

Songs My Mother Taught Me

There was nothing there for me to disbelieve.
—RANDALL JARRELL

Dvorak's "Songs My Mother Taught Me,"
From the cycle *Gypsy Melodies*, anticipates
The sonorous emotions of the Trio in F Minor,
Though without the latter's complications.
The melody is simple, while the piece's
Mood looks backwards, carried by the sweet,
Sustaining rhythms of the mother's voice
Embodied in the figure of the violin, until,
Upon the second repetition of the theme
And on a high, protracted note, it suddenly
Evaporates, while the piano lingers underneath.
The world remains indifferent to our needs,
Unchanged by what the mind, in its attempt to
Render it in terms that it can recognize,
Imagines it to be. The notes make up a story
Set entirely in the kingdom of appearance,
Filled with images of happiness and sadness
And projected on a place from which all
Evidence of what happened once has vanished—
A deserted cabin on a lake, or an isolated
Field in which two people walked together,
Or the nondescript remains of someone's home.
The place endures, unmindful and unseen,
Until its very absence comes to seem a shape

That seems to stand for something—a schematic
Face that floats above a background made of
Words that someone spoke, from which the human
Figure gradually emerges, like a shifting pattern
Drifting through a filigree of flimsy clouds
Above the massive, slowly turning globe.
Beneath the trees, beneath the constellations
Drawn from the illusions sketched by sight,
The tiny figures move in twos and threes
To their particular conclusions, like the details
Of a vision that, for all it leaves to see,
Might never have existed—its conviction spent,
Its separate shapes retracing an ascending
Curve of entropy, dissolving in that endless
Dream of physics, in which pain becomes unreal,
And happiness breaks down into its elements.

I wish there were an answer to that wish.
Why can't the unseen world—the real world—
Be like an aspect of a place that one remembers?
Why can't each thing present itself, and stay,
Without the need to be perfected or refined?
Why can't we live in some imaginary realm
Beyond belief, in which all times seem equal,
And without the space between the way things are
And how they merely seem? In which the minor,
Incidental shapes that meant the world to me
—That mean the world to me—are real too?
Suppose that time were nothing but erasure,
And that years were just whatever one had lost.

The things that managed to remain unchanged
Would seem inhuman, while the course life took
Would have a form that was too changeable to see.
The simple act of speech would make it true,
Yet at the cost of leaving nothing to believe.
Within this field, this child's imagination,
An entire universe could seem to flicker
In the span of one's attention, each succeeding
Vision mingling with the rest to form a tapestry
Containing multitudes, a wealth of incident
As various as the mind itself, yet ultimately
Composed of nothing but its mirror image:
An imaginary person, who remained, within that
Seamless web of supposition, utterly alone.

All this is preface. Last May my mother died
And I flew back to San Diego for her funeral.
Her life was uneventful, and the last ten
Years or so had seemed increasingly dependent
On a vague and doctrineless religion—a religion
Based on reassurance rather than redemption—
Filled with hopes so unspecific and a love so
Generalized that in the end it came to seem
A long estrangement, in the course of which those
Abstract sentiments had deepened and increased,
While all the real things—the things that
Used to seem so close I couldn't see them—
Had been burnished away by distance and by time,
Replaced by hazy recollections of contentment,
And obscured beneath a layer of association

Which had rendered them, once more, invisible.
And yet the streets still looked the same to me,
And even though the incidents seemed different,
The shapes that still remained exhibited the
Reassuring patterns of a natural order—
The quiet rhythms of a world demystified,
Without those old divisions into what was real
And what was wishful thinking. In a few days
Everything had altered, and yet nothing changed—
That was the anomalous event that happened
In the ordinary course of things, from which the
Rest of us were simply absent, or preoccupied,
Or busy with arrangements for the flowers,
The music, the reception at the house for various
Cousins, aunts and uncles and, from next door,
Mr. Palistini with his tooth of gold. At
Length the house was empty, and I went outside.
It struck me that this place, which overnight
Had almost come to seem a part of me, was actually
The same one I had longed for years to leave.
There were differences of course—another
House or two, and different cars—and yet what
Startled me was how familiar it all seemed—
The numbers stenciled on the curb, the soap dish
In the bathroom, the boxes still in the garage—
As though the intricate evasions of the years
Had left their underlying forms unchanged.
And this is not to say those fables were untrue,
But merely that their spells were incomplete—
Incomplete and passing. For although we can't

Exist without our fantasies, at times they
Start to come apart like clouds, to leave us
Momentarily alone, within an ordinary setting—
Disenchanted and alone, but also strangely free,
And suddenly relieved to find a vast, inhuman
World, completely independent of our lives
And yet behind them all, still there.

The Realm of Ends

I wish there were a state of being
Of a different kind, not compromised
And caught between the twin extremes of
Something inconceivable and something else
Untrue; between the overarching heavens
And the merely human. Some things are
Not to be sought after in reality, not
Even in the mind, but in a hidden region
Where the soul is free and unrestrained
And thought proceeds like weightless
Stars across an unseen sky. Oh yes, I
Realize this inner paradise is just, like
Time, or other worlds or selves impossibly
Remote or deep within, another intimate
Illusion on the border of intelligence,
A thing you have to touch and brush away,
Because nothing is hidden. These heavens
Are the only ones there are, an all-inclusive
Frame displaying every aspect of the real
Against an infinite night sky the thick,
Dark, translucent color of obsidian. Yet
In the wakefulness that comes towards dawn I
Still sometimes think of myself—in a style of
Thinking whose trajectory must have once seemed
Clear, but which now seems loose, strange, and

Difficult to follow—as somehow distant from a
Universe of merely changing things, eternal
In the way each moment is, and free, the
Way each star becomes increasingly
Elusive once it crosses the meridian.

Argument in Isolation

Premise: one exists alone,
Within a system of increasingly mild ideals
—The good of love, the greater good of dreams—
Abstracted from the musings of the grown-up child

That somewhere, in a scene above the sky,
Lies smiling. Anxious to begin
Before the will can answer and its passions fly away
Like sparrows, he lays aside his cares and

Lets the world come, lets its shapes return,
Its mirrors answer and its angels roam across the narrow
Confines of the page. Like friends
Estranged by distance and the inwardness of age,

The spaces between letters become spaces between lives,
The fact of pain begins to seem unreal, the trees
Begin to seem too distant; the imaginary self,
Concealed from the world, begins its cry

Yet remains empty—as though it could contain
No tenderness beyond its own, and no other love
Than that concealed in its own reflection, hovering
On the threshold of age, between two lives.

Premise: the world and the mind are one,
With a single splendor. And to say the way a
Street looked, or the way the light fell in a canyon,
Is to realize the way time feels in passing, as

The will to change becomes the effort to remember,
And then a passive sigh. An eidolon
Constructed out of air, grown out of nothing,
Planted at the center of a space shaped like a heart,

The tree in Eden spreads its leaves against the sun,
While in its shade, as evening starts to fall,
One hears the cry that comes to seem one's own. When
All the fantasies are done, the songs have ended

And the arguments begun in isolation have concluded,
Something effortless remains, that finds its measure in the sky.
The mind survives its disappointments
In the way that time creates a vision of the real

To soothe its passage, nourishing what it sees,
Then melding with it in a luminous, transparent scene
Made up in equal parts by how the world might look
From heaven, and on an ordinary day.

—That is the burden of the argument:
Things change, love fades, life comes undone,
And yet the need for everything remains.
I wanted to create a logic of the soul

౿

In which the mind could seal its treasures
And part of my imaginary childhood could survive.
These things you read are part of a design
As intricate as reason and intangible as time

That hides the themes of living in its coils.
I think the truest language is the one translated by the leaves
When the wind blows through them, and the truest
Statement is the one asserted by the sun

That shines indifferently on loneliness and love;
And that neither one is bearable. Like wings
That let the speaker soar above his state
Into the welcoming arms of care, the unacknowledged

Hunger draws its consolations from the air,
From dreams, and from the quiet sweetness it identifies with love.
Yet nothing answers, and the only presence is a page
Which remains silent, and there is no one there.

Sometimes I wish the world would vanish into space,
Leaving me alone in my imagination.
Sometimes I wonder if this love I claim to feel
Is just a wish that someone else's life seem like my own,

Or that another person's emotions feel like mine.
But mostly I just marvel at the way mere time
Can make a life seem nonexistent, sweep the soul away,
And leave the world as though a person hadn't really lived in it at all.

☙

These arguments contest that disappearance.
Does it even matter whether anyone is listening?
Even if the light should fail, their tenderness prove illusory
And the transcendental child grow old and die,

Their fallacies would still evoke a kind of history,
A demonstration of the years spent waiting,
Echoing the reply I knew was never going to come,
Not simply as an exercise in isolation,

But as solace for this life of quietly existing,
In the traces left behind by love, until the light holds,
And the world and the mind are one.
One exists alone.

The Third Wish

The first two expressed hope, but after that
A feeling of desperation set in,
Because nothing had happened. Once again,
Tomorrow faded out into the flat,

Monotonous drone of a radio
Playing next door *"Dream / When you're feeling blue"*
As all night long they deepened and came true
Invisibly, so that no one should know.

Everyone knew that the story ended
With someone waiting, followed by a sigh;
That the refined pleasures got replaced by
Sentimental torch songs, the once splendid

Gardens choked with nightmare weeds, while a tame
Ghost flitted through the mansion like a sad
Delusion of the grandeur it had once had.
Yet the end, when it finally came, came

Unexpectedly, like a piece of mail
From that country where the dark flowers bloomed
That started lightly, but quickly assumed
The tenor of a cautionary tale

ᔕ

Set in Cloud–Cuckoo–Land, whose official
Moral was patience, but whose real message
Was left obscure, like a rite of passage
Into the realm of the artificial.

It was a funny kind of parable
Though, since Everyman was a memory
And the hero someone who couldn't see
Beyond himself, despite the terrible

Soul inexorably gravitating
Towards him like a malignant soap bubble,
With the smooth, dead features of his double,
And a voice that kept insinuating

Danger, because something had come too near
And ordinary emotions, like hate,
Had become impossible to translate,
Living within the diminishing fear

Of death and the innumerable ways
Of waiting, of feeling time pass from now
To never, and then discovering how
In another life, or in a few days.

Friends

for David Schatz

Picnics in the woods behind the Institute;
Evenings in the garden at Madoo, or the farm in Spring Green;
The loft on Prince Street; four apartments in Chelsea
And Cambridge, and the house in Sarasota—

These used to make the world seem feasible and small,
As though the shape it took, and what the future would hold,
Could be composed of what the past already knew,
And contained within the covers of an address book.

It isn't still a premise, or that central thing
That E. M. Forster once hoped he might betray his country for.
It isn't—to use that awful word—a "value" anymore.
Yet people live in one another's minds,

In one another's company at dinner, in the annual,
Late-night calls on New Year's Eve. Scared of being alone,
Alone at the end; gathering the remnants of those singular
     occasions
Like a cloak or a shawl, drawing its raveled sleeve

Against a universe oblivious to care—
Is *this* how friendship tends? Where affection leads?
Night falls behind a screen of willow trees
And on the upland pasture, where their wistful images abide,

Sidling into view, brightening for a moment
Through the terrifying sheen around the narrow corridor of sight,
As the years narrow into a lengthening corridor of
Absence, and the darkness of their absence.

The Secret Amplitude

I

Perhaps the hardest feeling is the one
Of unrealized possibility:
Thoughts left unspoken, actions left undone

That seemed to be of little consequence
To things considered in totality;
And yet that might have made a difference.

Sometimes the thought of what one might have done
Starts to exhaust the life that it explains,
After so much of what one knew has gone.

I guess that all things happen for the best,
And that whatever life results remains,
In its own fashion, singularly blest.

Yet when I try to I think about the ways
That brought me here, I think about places
Visited, about particular days

Whiled away with a small handful of friends,
Some of them gone; and about the traces
Of a particular movement, that ends

෨

In mild effects, but that originates
In the sheer "wonder of disappointment,"
Ascending in an arc that resonates

Through the heavens, before a dying fall.
I don't know what Wittgenstein might have meant
By *nothing is hidden*, if not that all

The aspects of one's life are there to see.
But last month, coming back on the *métro*
From the basilica of St. Denis,

My sense of here and now began to melt
Into a sensation of vertigo
I realized that I had never felt.

II

Start with the condition of the given:
A room, a backyard, or a city street.
Next, construct an idea of heaven

By eliminating the contingent
Accidents that make it seem familiar.
Spanning these polarities—the stringent

Vacuum and the sound of a lawnmower—
Find the everyday experiences
Making up our lives, set on the lower

Branches of the tree of knowledge. Is *this*
What people mean by living in the world?
A region of imaginary bliss,

Uncontaminated by reflection,
Rationalized by the controlling thought
Of simple beauty, of the perfection

Of the commonplace through acquiescence?
Think of a deeper order of beauty,
A kind of magnificence whose essence

Lies in estrangement, the anxiety
Of the unrecognized, in resistance,
And in the refusal of piety.

❧

Nothing comes of nothing: what ideals
Alter is the look of things, the changing
Surfaces their argument reveals

To be illusory. Yet one still *tries*,
Pulled inward by the promissory thought
Of something time can never realize,

Both inexhaustible and self-contained;
Of something waiting to be discovered
In the dominion of the unattained.

III

I always think about it in a way
So inflected by the thought of places,
And of my distance from them; by other

People, and the measure of another
Year since they departed, that they get hard
To separate, like the thought of a day

From the day itself. I suppose the proof,
If there is one, is by analogy
With the kind of adolescent "knowledge"

I had on those afternoons in college
When I'd go to New York, and the evening
Deepened, and then the lights came on. Aloof,

Yet somehow grounded in the real, it's
Like an abstract diagram of a face,
Or the experience of memory

Drained of its vivifying imagery
—Of Geoff's cigars, for instance, or Willy's
Collision with the pillar at the Ritz—

Until the pure experience remains.
For over time, the personal details
Came to mean less to me than the feeling

∾

Of simply having lived them, revealing
Another way of being in the world,
With all the inwardness it still sustains,

And the promise of happiness it brought.
So it began to take over my life—
Not like some completely arbitrary

Conception someone had imposed on me,
But more and more like a second nature;
Until it became my abiding thought.

IV

How much can someone actually retain
Of a first idea? What the day was,
Or what the flowers in the room were like,

Or how the curtains lifted in the breeze?
The meaning lies in what a person does
In the aftermath of that abundance,

On an ordinary day in August
In the still air, beneath a milk-white sky—
As something quickens in the inner room

No one inhabits, filling its domain
With the sound of an ambiguous sigh
Muffled by traffic noises. Underneath,

The movement starts to recapitulate
Another season and another life,
Walking through the streets of Barcelona,

Its alleys and its accidents combined
Into an arabesque of feeling, rife
With imprecision, blending everything

Into a song intended to obscure,
Like the song of the wind, and so begin
To repeat the fallacy of the past:

෴

That it was pure, and that the consummate
Endeavor is to bring it back again.
Would it make any difference? Each breath

Anticipates the next, until the end.
Nothing lasts. The imperative of change
Is what the wind repeats, and night brings dreams

Illuminating the transforming thought
Of the familiar context rendered strange,
The displacement of the ordinary.

V

I hadn't been to Paris in six years.
My hotel room was like a pleasant cell.
On the plane I'd been bothered by vague fears

Of being by myself for the first time,
Or recognizing the sound of the bell
Of Saint-Germain-des-Prés, or a street mime

At Deux Magots, and being overwhelmed
By the sensation of being alone.
Even with a friend, from the distant realm

Of Rome, I couldn't shake the impression
Of exile, as though I'd come to atone
For some indescribable transgression—

A state of anonymity, without
Anonymity's deep sense of pardon.
We ate, and walked about, and talked about

The true nature of the sentimental.
Later, as I imagined the garden
Of the new Bibliothèque Nationale

Drowsing in its shade of information,
I felt the peace of insignificance,
Of a solitude like a vocation

❧

To be inhabited, to be explored
With the single-minded perseverance
Of a blind man whose sight had been restored.

Everything seemed so mindless and abstract,
Stripped of the personality I knew.
The evening was like a secret compact,

And though it was May, the night air felt cold.
The sky was black. The sky was gold and blue
Above an Eiffel Tower lit with gold.

VI

What is the abstract, the impersonal?
Are they the same? And whence this grandiose
Geography of a few emotions?

Think of an uninhabited landscape,
With its majesty rendered otiose
By a stranger's poverty of feeling;

Then contemplate that state without a name
In which something formless and inchoate
Stirs in an act of definition, like

A thought becoming conscious of itself,
For which the words are always late, too late.
The motion spreads its shape across the sky,

Unburdened by causality and death.
Where is that paradise? Where is that womb
Of the unreal, that expansiveness

That turned the mountains into vacant air,
The empty desert to an empty tomb
On Sunday, with the body set aside,

The sense of diminution giving way,
Through the oscillations of the sublime,   ·
To an infinite expanse of spirit?

∽

If only one could know, at this remove,
The private alchemy, obscured by time,
By which an inhospitable terrain

Became an open space, "a fresh, green breast"
Of a new world of such magnificence
That those who entered were as though reborn,

And everything they heard and saw and felt
Melted into shape and significance;
And what that secret amplitude was like.

VII

But is there even anything to know?
Linger over the cases: the dead friends,
And what the obituaries omit

And one can only imagine: what *it*
Must have felt like at the end, suspended
Between two impossible tasks, as though

The burden of each day were to rebut
A presumption of disillusionment
And a sense of hopelessness, deflected

By the daily routine, yet protected
By the cave of the imagination;
Until at last the inner door slammed shut.

When did it all become unbearable?
The question begs the questions of their lives
Asked from the inside, taking for granted

Their very being, as though enchanted
By the way the settings, in retrospect,
Make up the logic of a parable

Whose incidents make no sense, and by how
Time tries to project a kind of order,
And the terrifying clarity it brings,

༄

Into the enigma of the last things—
A vodka bottle lying on the floor,
An off-hand remark ("I'll be going now")—

With everything contained, as in a proof,
In a few emblems of finality:
The bullet in the mouth. The sharp report

That no one else can hear. The sharp report
That only someone else *could* hear. The long,
Irrevocable transport from the roof.

VIII

If God in Heaven were a pair of eyes
Whose gaze could penetrate the camouflage
Of speech and thought, the innocent disguise

Of a person looking in the mirror;
If a distant mind, in its omniscience,
Could reflect and comprehend the terror

Obscured by the trappings of the body—
If these possibilities were real,
Everything would look the same: a cloudy

Sky low in the distance, and a dead tree
Visible through the window. The same thoughts
Would engage the mind: that one remains free

In a limited sense, and that the rough
Approximation of eternity
Contained in every moment is enough.

What sponsors the idea of a god
Magnificent in its indifference,
And inert above the shabby, slipshod

Furnishings that constitute the human?
What engenders the notion of a state
Transcending the familiar, common

ᴄᴐ

Ground on which two people walked together
Some twenty years ago, through a small park?
The benches remain empty. The weather

Changes with the seasons, which feel the same.
The questions trace out the trajectory
Of a person traveling backwards, whose name

Occupies a space between death and birth;
Of someone awkwardly celebrating
A few diminished angels, and the earth.

IX

It's been nine years since the telephone call
From Mark, and a year since the one from John.
And it's as though nothing's *changed*, but that all

The revisions were finally over.
And yet now more than half my life is gone,
Like those years of waiting to discover

That hidden paradise of the recluse
I was always just about to enter—
Until it came to seem like an excuse

For the evasion of intimacy.
At Willy's memorial last winter,
Edward Albee spoke of his privacy,

And how at last he wandered up the stairs
To a "final privacy." And perhaps
The illusions that keep us from our cares

Are projections of our mortality,
Of the impulse inside the fear it maps
Onto the sky, while in reality

The fear continues underneath. I guess
That despite the moments of resplendence
Like the one in Paris, it's still the less

❧

Insistent ones that come to rest within.
I don't know why the thought of transcendence
Beckons us, or why we strive for it in

Solitary gestures of defiance,
Or try to discover it in our dreams,
Or by rending the veil of appearance.

Why does it have to issue from afar?
Why can't we find it in the way life *seems*?
As Willy would have said—*So, here we are.*

The Interior of the Future

The windows will be lighted, not the rooms.
—WALLACE STEVENS

Sheathed in copper-colored glass, its featureless facade
Reflects the green patina of the cone-shaped roof of City Hall.
The building dominates a stretch of Water Street
That wanders past some tanneries, rising towards the old Italian
   neighborhood
Set on a low hill, and sloping down to where the river flows
Under the North Avenue bridge, by a dam and desultory
   waterfall.
The highways stream insensibly away. Miles to the north,
Beneath the unencumbered, transsuburban skies
And the sound of elevator music; in the melancholy sunlight at
   the edge of town,
The numbers sleep inside a dreaming abstract city,
A disenfranchised zone—the inverse image of a neighborhood—
Of office parks and towers with enigmatic names, obscurer
   purposes,
All scattered here and there across the half-developed fields
Like tombstones in the graveyard of the common good,
Whose windows replicate the smooth, autistic surface of the
   sepulcher downtown.
If you should come this way—if you should wander out alone
Some summer afternoon, en route to meet a realtor, or a friend,
Or simply looking for a magazine—you might experience the
   disconcerting sense

Of having wandered through a place like this before
Without recognizing it, as though a face you knew you knew felt
    unfamiliar.
The sky is still the same unearthly blue. Illuminated signs repeat
The stock quotations hour by hour. Enchanted by its past,
Oblivious to what the future holds, the city hovers in its mirror of
    illusions,
As a beer truck makes its way across the bridge above the dam,
And the traffic comes and goes on Water Street.

A figure in a landscape: strip the artifacts away
And leave a habitat composed of water, trees, and glaciated soil.
Conceive a seamless blend of hunger, reverie, and feeling
Bound together in a smooth, unviolated orb.
Phase two: the unformed innocent peers out at what controls it
    from afar.
Phase three goes on forever, winding backwards in an interlocking
    coil
Of impulse and perception, memory and the vestiges of fear.
There is a fable of the soul as self-contained,
Taking its measures from within, without a glance at its
    surroundings.
Yet the image in the heart is of a bare, unstructured plain,
Drawn outwards by the flame of its imprisoning milieu,
To be extinguished in a space it both engenders and absorbs.
Clouds, and the dilution of desire. The sigh you seem to hear
As the treetops bend against the wind, and the sidewalks glisten in
    the rain.
There is a balance of effect, as if each sound, each faintly nuanced
    hue

Contained a single shade of feeling, and the movements of
    emotion through the mind
Threw shadows on the walls, and made the windows shimmer
    from within.
And as the vagueness at its core is rendered clear,
An entity emerges from the forms experience provides: a domicile
    at first,
But then a neighborhood, a town, a fantasy of states, a country.
Rising through the air, the individual's story left behind
Like photographs abandoned in the corner of a drawer,
Its outline merges with the outlines of abandoned buildings
Seen from a remote height, from high above the surface of a
    sphere,
As though bare fields could have a kind of structure too.

The lake seems unperturbed. The streets were still deserted
As I rode my bike down Water Tower Hill, then south along the
    drive
And towards an alabaster city gleaming through the haze,
Like a quiet hallucination in the morning sun. On the news last
    night
There was a segment on the city of the future: an enclave of
    illuminated shells
Encircled by a no-man's-land of disaffected lives,
Where people puzzled to themselves in isolation, fleshing out their
    days
With fantasies of what a home was like, or what the future held.
Coming back I made a circuit through Lake Park,
Lingering for a moment on a bridge above a deep ravine
Between some limestone lions guarding the approach at either end.

I caught glimpses of the water through the trees;
Overhead, an unseen airplane dragged a trail across the sky.
What *is* the soul, if not the space in which it lives writ small?
There is a balance of exchanges, like a voice descanting in the dark
While outside, in the bright arena of July, a band is playing.
There passed across my mind a morning forty years ago,
When I lay in bed and watched the sunlight deepen on the wall.
Why did the balance have to alter? I feel swept forward on a self-
    effacing wave,
As the bindings of the commonplace give way, and the world goes
    slack.
The traffic floats along the drive. The people come and go
As in an elevator rising through the lobby of a new hotel
Into a frame of mind, a future state whose story lies beyond recall
In a maze of speculation, a vast network of transactions
On an enormous grid, but not a country anymore. I want it back.

Morning in America

It gradually became a different country
After the reversal, dominated by a distant,
Universal voice whose favorite word was *never*,
Changing its air of quiet progress into one of
Rapidly collapsing possibilities, and making me,
Even here at home, a stranger. I felt its tones
Engaging me without expression, leaving me alone
And waiting in the vacuum of its public half-life,
Quietly confessing my emotions, taking in its cold
Midwinter atmosphere of violence and muted rage. I
Wanted to appropriate that anger, to convey it, not
In a declamatory mode, but in some vague and private
Language holding out, against the clear, inexorable
Disintegration of a nation, the claims of a renewed
Internal life, in these bleak months of the new year.
That was my way of ruling out everything discordant,
Everything dead, cruel, or soulless—by assiduously
Imagining the pages of some legendary volume marked
Forever, but without ever getting any closer. As I
Got older it began to seem more and more hopeless,
More and more detached—until it only spoke to me
Impersonally, like someone gradually retreating,
Not so much from his life as from its settings,
From the country he inhabits; as the darkness
Deepens in the weeks after the solstice.

A Pathetic Landscape

The purpose remains constant: to change a
Pretense of description into one of feeling,
And to translate the face of the external world
Into a language spoken in the mind, and with

The inward eye survey the frozen aspects of a
Wilderness illuminated by a cold, imaginary sun.
Somehow these artifacts, which come to next to
Nothing on their own, collectively define a

Discourse of the individual, vibrating with a
Solipsistic rhetoric sustained by a succession of
Minute, spectacular effects, and even superficially
Alive; yet finally incomplete, its terms confined

To this austere, conversational vernacular. What
Is plain language anyway? Is it the one you think,
Or hear, or one that you imagine? Can it incorporate
The numinous as well as the particular, and the ways

Ideas move, and the aftertaste that a conviction leaves
Once its strength has faded? I don't believe it anymore,
But I can hear it sighing in the wind, and feel it in the
Movement of the leaves outside my window as the season

∽

Deepens into ice and silence. It speaks too slowly,
While the sentiments it once could bring to life feel
Dissipated now, the blood runs colder in the veins,
This room in which I live seems smaller every day

And every time I hear those tones of voice that
Used to mean the world to me, and which will not
Come back to me again, even the wind turns bitter
And the clouds stream furiously across the sun.

Early Morning in Milwaukee

Is this what I was made for? Is the world that fits
Like what I feel when I wake up each morning? Steamclouds
Hovering over the lake, and smoke ascending from ten thousand
    chimneys
As in a picture on a calendar, in a frieze of ordinary days?
Beneath a sky of oatmeal gray, the land slides downward from a
    K-mart parking lot
Into a distance lined with bungalows, and then a vague horizon.
Higher and higher, until its gaze becomes a part of what it sees,
The mind ascends through layers of immobility into an unfamiliar
    atmosphere
Where nothing lives, and with a sense of finally breaking free
Attains its kingdom: a constructed space, or an imaginary city
Bordered all around by darkness; or a city gradually sinking into
    age,
Dominated by a television tower whose blue light warns the
    traveler away.

People change, or drift away, or die. It used to be a country
Bounded by possibility, from which the restless could embark
And then come home to, and where the soul could find an
    emblem of itself.
Some days I feel a momentary lightness, but then the density
    returns,
The salt-encrusted cars drive by the factory where a clock tower
Overlooks the highway, and the third shift ends. And then softly,
The way the future used to sing to me when I was ten years old,
I start to hear the murmur of a voice that isn't mine at all,

46

Formless and indistinct, the music of a world that holds no place
     for me;
And then an image starts to gather in my mind—a picture of a
     room
Where someone lingers at a window, staring at a nearly empty
     street
Bordered by freight yards and abandoned tanneries. And then the
     bus stops
And a man gets off, and stands still, and then walks away.

Last night I had a dream in which the image of a long-forgotten
     love
Hovered over the city. No one could remember what his name
     was
Or where he came from, or decipher what that emptiness might
     mean;
Yet on the corner, next to the *USA Today* machine, a woman
     seemed to wave at me,
Until the stream of morning traffic blocked her from my view.
It's strange, the way a person's life can feel so far away,
Although the claims of its existence are encountered everywhere
—In a drugstore, or on the cover of a tabloid, on the local news
Or in the mail that came this morning, in the musings of some
     talk show host
Whose face is an enigma and whose name is just a number in the
     phone book,
But whose words are as pervasive as the atmosphere I breathe.
Why can't I find my name in this profusion? Nothing even
     stays,
No image glances back at me, no inner angel hurls itself in rage

Against the confines of this surface that confronts me everywhere
    I look
—At home or far away, here or on the way back from the store—
Behind an all-inclusive voice and personality, fashioned out of fear
And scattered like a million isolated points transmitting random
    images
Across a space alive with unconnected signals.

                                        I heard my name
Once, but then the noise of waiting patiently resumed. It felt the
    same,
Yet gradually the terms I used to measure out my life increased,
Until I realized that I'd been driving down these streets for sixteen
    years.
I was part of the surroundings: people looked at me the way I used
    to look at them,
And most of what I felt seemed second nature. Now and then
    that sense I'd had in high school
—Of a puzzlement about to lift, a language just about to start—
Meandered into consciousness; but by and large I'd spend the days
Like something in the background, or like part of a design too
    intricate to see.
Wasn't there supposed to be a stage at which the soul at last broke
    free
And started to meet the world on equal terms? To feel a little
    more at home,
More intensely realized, more successfully contained
Within the arc of its achievements? Filled with reservations,
Moods and private doubts, yet always moving, with increasing
    confidence,

Towards a kind of summary, towards the apex of a long career
Advancing down an avenue that opened on a space of sympathy
    and public understanding?
Or howling like the wind in the wires outside my window, in a
    cacophony of rage?
I don't think so. Age is like the dreams one had in childhood,
Some parts of which *were* true—I have the things I want, the
    words to misdescribe them,
And the freedom to imagine what I think I feel. I think that most
    of what I feel remains unknown,
But that beneath my life lies something intricate and real and
Nearly close enough to touch. I live it, and I know I should
    explain it,
Only I know I can't—it's just an image of my life that came to me
    one day,
And which remained long after the delight it brought had ended.
Sometimes I think I hear the sound of death approaching
Like a song in the trees, a performance staged for me and me
    alone
And written in the ersatz language of loss, the language of time
    passing,
Or the sound of someone speaking decorously into the unknown
—Like a voice picked up on the telephone when two lines cross
    momentarily
—Overheard, and then half-heard, and then gone.

Henrietta

In some small town, one indifferent summer.
—JOHN ASHBERY

The limitless blue sky is still a page
Beyond imagination. The incidental
Clouds traverse it as they did in 1933,
Or above Pearl Harbor, or above the
Outskirts of a prosperous North Texas town
When both of my grandparents were young.
April frosts the trees with green,
The flowers start to blossom in the shade,
And as the seasons come around again
The unsung melody resumes above the leaves—
Emotionless and free, its character unmarked by time,
As though a century had opened just an hour ago.
The terms our lives propose elude them,
And the underlying themes that bind them into wholes
Are difficult to hear inside an isolated room—
Receding, like the memory of a particular afternoon
That flickers like a smile across the quiet face of time,
Into private history. And my father's parents
Stumble through the Crash into an unfamiliar world
With no relation to the one they'd had in mind—
As in certain parlor games, or manipulated photographs,
In which the intricate details of individual lives
Dissolve into the accidental shapes that they compose.

Sometimes the ordinary light stops shining,
And the sky above the bungalows takes on the dull,
Metallic sheen of some premonitory gong
Suspended high above our cares, above our lives.
The grand piano in the living room,
The antimacassars on the damasked chairs—
Sometimes their distant counterpoint returns,
As though diurnal time had halted, and the street
Were like a boulevard illuminated by the moon
Or bathed in the dim aquarium light of an eclipse.
The birds know it, and from deep inside
The rooms seem lit with echoes of the faint,
Unearthly music that from time to time one hears
Beneath the incidental music of the human—
The disenchanting music of indifference;
Of the dark, indifferent spheres.

When I was seven or eight my father
Drove us all half-way across the country
In an emerald Chevrolet with benchlike seats
To visit my grandparents in Texas.
The coastal vegetation gradually gave way
To an interminable, scrub-filled desert,
Rhyming lines of signs for Burma-Shave,
And railroad tracks with wooden water towers.
The house was cavernous and cool and clean,
With a pecan tree in the backyard, and flowers
Set along the side that faced a rudimentary swing.
Lincrusta Walton walls, the tubular brass bed
Where my grandfather kept snoring as I tried to sleep—

For all that I can see, these things weren't real,
And yet their vestiges have managed to survive
As on a hidden stream, and with a logic of their own,
Like minor histories made up from vagrant
Images that seem to roam at random in your mind,
Or thoughts your memory carries on its light,
Rejuvenating breeze, that brings them back to life
With an intensity they never had in life—
The images of Nana's hair and Bobby's glasses
Floating in an atmosphere of fading mental
Snapshots of a miniature downtown, and rows of
Dark cars parked diagonally by the sidewalks,
And the barber shop he opened after the bank collapsed.
After my grandmother died, he stayed on for a while
In their unlocked house, amid her "lovely things"
—The candlesticks, the sparkling cut-crystal bowls—
That strangers wandered in and stole. When
We returned, he'd moved into a little bungalow
Next to some open fields, which he and I methodically
Patrolled on Sundays in his dull black Ford,
Shooting birds and rabbits with a .410 shotgun.
He died my freshman year in college.
Last week, when I was back in California,
My father talked about the pleasure he'd derived
From his collection of fine guns, which were
Among the few things that he'd taken when he moved,
And which, while he lay dying in the hospital
During his final illness, were stolen too.

☙

A writer's secret is an uncorrupted world.
Nobody lives there, and the intricate affairs
Of state, or those of day-to-day existence
Wait undreamed of; while their echoes
Slide into a residue of multiple erasures.
Reading all this over, I have the sense
That what I've just described was just a pretext,
And that what I really meant was something
Utterly removed from Henrietta and the little
Stories I remember. Like an unmarked page,
One's universe extends beyond its comprehending mind,
And what had seemed so momentarily clear
In its eternal instant, flickers into obscurity
Along the dull, unwritten passages of time.
The penitent rests his case. My father
Finished college, left home for a conservatory,
And played with orchestras in Europe and New York
Until the war came and he joined the Navy.
What *are* years? Their shapes accelerate and blur
Into an outline of my life, into this specious
Present I can find no words for, whose
Extent is recollection and the patterns that it
Throws upon the firmament of widely scattered stars,
On the inscrutable dark matter at its core.
The soul invents a story of its passing,
Yet the fables it creates, like chamber music,
Float through half-remembered rooms, where someone
Waits at a piano, or some open fields in Texas,
Where a train rolls by and clouds drift slowly overhead.
I said I thought the real song lay deeper,

Yet its words are snatches of those adolescent tunes
That wax and wane at random, as one lies in bed
Before the healing wave of sleep; or while one lingers
Outside on a summer evening, with a dazzling canopy of stars
Surrounding a mind like a jar full of fireflies.
The metaphors that amplify the one we call the world
Are surface eddies, while the underlying stream
Endures below the frequency of consciousness,
Like the inaudible sensation of a buried organ note
That seems to issue from within. The rest
Is merely speculation, fading from one's attention
Like the diary of a dream recorded years and years ago,
And apprehended from the vantage point of age
—And the only real vantage point *is* age—
That seems at first too close, and then too clear,
But ultimately of no real concern at all.
I guess what finally keeps the time are just these
Chronicles of the smaller worlds—the private
Journals, the chronologies that span the century,
While something lurks beyond their borders,
Beyond our power to imagine: an elementary state
Unshaped by feeling, uncorrupted by experience
And converging on an old, impersonal ideal
Bereft of human features, whose enigmatic face
Still broods behind the sky above the town—
Inert and beautiful, but with the permanence of an idea
Too remote from us, and too tangible to retrieve.

Falling Water

I drove to Oak Park, took two tours,
And looked at some of the houses.
I took the long way back along the lake.
The place that I came home to—a cavernous
Apartment on the East Side of Milwaukee—
Seems basically a part of that tradition,
With the same admixture of expansion and restraint:
The space takes off, yet leaves behind a nagging
Feeling of confinement, with the disconcerting sense
That while the superficial conflicts got resolved,
The underlying tensions brought to equilibrium,
It isn't yet a place in which I feel that I can live.
Imagine someone reading. Contemplate a man
Oblivious to his settings, and then a distant person
Standing in an ordinary room, hemmed in by limitations,
Yet possessed by the illusion of an individual life
That blooms within its own mysterious enclosure,
In a solitary space in which the soul can breathe
And where the heart can stay—not by discovering it,
But by creating it, by giving it a self-sustaining
Atmosphere of depth, both in the architecture,
And in the unconstructed life that it contains.
In a late and very brief remark, Freud speculates
That space is the projection of a "psychic apparatus"
Which remains almost entirely oblivious to itself;
And Wright extols "that primitive sense of shelter"
Which can turn a house into a refuge from despair.
I wish that time could bring the future back again

And let me see things as they used to seem to me
Before I found myself alone, in an emancipated state—
Alone and free and filled with cares about tomorrow.
There used to be a logic in the way time passed
That made it flow directly towards an underlying space
Where all the minor, individual lives converged.
The moments borrowed their perceptions from the past
And bathed the future in a soft, familiar light
I remembered from home, and which has faded.
And the voices get supplanted by the rain,
The nights seem colder, and the angel in the mind
That used to sing to me beneath the wide suburban sky
Turns into dreamwork and dissolves into the air,
While in its place a kind of monument appears,
Magnificent in isolation, compromised by proximity
And standing in a small and singular expanse—
As though the years had been a pretext for reflection,
And my life had a been phase of disenchantment—
As the faces that I cherished gradually withdraw,
The reassuring settings slowly melt away,
And what remains is just a sense of getting older.
In a variation of the parable, the pure of heart
Descend into a kingdom that they never wanted
And refused to see. The homely notions of the good,
The quaint ideas of perfection swept away like
Adolescent fictions as the real forms of life
Deteriorate with manically increasing speed,
The kind man wakes into a quiet dream of shelter,
And the serenity it brings—not in reflection,
But in the paralyzing fear of being mistaken,

Of losing everything, of acquiescing in the
Obvious approach (the house shaped like a box;
The life that can't accommodate another's)—
As the heart shrinks down to tiny, local things.

Why can't the more expansive ecstasies come true?
I met you more than thirty years ago, in 1958,
In Mrs. Wolford's eighth grade history class.
All moments weigh the same, and matter equally;
Yet those that time brings back create the fables
Of a happy or unsatisfying life, of minutes
Passing on the way to either peace or disappointment—
Like a paper calendar on which it's always autumn
And we're back in school again; or a hazy afternoon
Near the beginning of October, with the World Series
Playing quietly on the radio, and the windows open,
And the California sunlight filling up the room.
When I survey the mural stretched across the years
—Across my heart—I notice mostly small, neglected
Parts of no importance to the whole design, but which,
In their obscurity, seem more permanent and real.
I see the desks and auditorium, suffused with
Yellow light connoting earnestness and hope that
Still remains there, in a space pervaded by a
Soft and supple ache too deep to contemplate—
As though the future weren't real, and the present
Were amorphous, with nothing to hold on to,
And the past were there forever. And the art
That time inflicts upon its subjects can't
Eradicate the lines sketched out in childhood,

Which harden into shapes as it recedes.
I wish I knew a way of looking at the world
That didn't find it wanting, or of looking at my
Life that didn't always see a half-completed
Structure made of years and filled with images
And gestures emblematic of the past, like Gatsby's
Light, or Proust's imbalance on the stones.
I wish there were a place where I could stay
And leave the world alone—an enormous stadium
Where I could wander back and forth across a field
Replete with all the incidents and small details
That gave the days their textures, that bound the
Minutes into something solid, and that linked them
All together in a way that used to seem eternal.
We used to go to dances in my family's ancient
Cadillac, which blew up late one summer evening
Climbing up the hill outside Del Mar. And later
I can see us steaming off the cover of the Beatles'
Baby-butcher album at your house in Mission Bay;
And three years later listening to the Velvet
Underground performing in a roller skating rink.
Years aren't texts, or anything *like* texts;
And yet I often think of 1968 that way, as though
That single year contained the rhythms of the rest,
As what began in hope and eagerness concluded in
Intractable confusion, as the wedding turned into a
Puzzling fiasco over poor John Godfrey's hair.
The parts were real, and yet the dense and living
Whole they once composed seems broken now, its
Voice reduced to disembodied terms that speak to me

More distantly each day, until the tangled years
Are finally drained of feeling, and collapse into a
Sequence of the places where we lived: your parents'
House in Kensington, and mine above the canyon;
Then the flat by Sears in Cambridge, where we
Moved when we got married, and the third floor
Of the house on Francis Avenue, near Harvard Square;
The big apartment in Milwaukee where we lived the
Year that John was born, and last of all the
House in Whitefish Bay, where you live now
And all those years came inexplicably undone
In mid-July. The sequence ended late last year.
Suppose we use a lifetime as a measure of the world
As it exists for one. Then half of mine has ended,
While the fragment which has recently come to be
Contains no vantage point from which to see it whole.
I think that people are the sum of their illusions,
That the cares that make them difficult to see
Are eased by distance, with their errors blending
In an intricate harmony, their truths abiding
In a subtle "spark" or psyche (each incomparable,
Yet each the same as all the others) and their
Disparate careers all joined together in a tangled
Moral vision whose intense, meandering design
Seems lightened by a pure simplicity of feeling,
As in grief, or in the pathos of a life
Cut off by loneliness, indifference or hate,
Because the most important thing is human happiness—
Not in the sense of private satisfactions, but of
Lives that realize themselves in ordinary terms

And with the quiet inconsistencies that make them real.
The whole transcends its tensions, like the intimate
Reflections on the day that came at evening, whose
Significance was usually overlooked, or misunderstood,
Because the facts were almost always unexceptional.
Two years ago we took our son to Paris. Last night
I picked him up and took him to a Lou Reed show,
And then took him home. I look at all the houses as I
Walk down Hackett Avenue to work. I teach my classes,
Visit friends, cook introspective meals for myself,
Yet in the end the minutes don't add up. What's lost
Is the perception of the world as something good
And held in common; as a place to be perfected
In the kinds of everyday divisions and encounters
That endowed it with integrity and structure,
And that merged its private moments with the past.
What broke it into pieces? What transformed the
Flaws that gave it feeling into objects of a deep and
Smoldering resentment—like coming home too early,
Or walking too far ahead of you on the rue Jacob?
I wish that life could be a window on the sun,
Instead of just this porch where I can stand and
Contemplate the wires that lace the parking lot
And feel it moving towards some unknown resolution.
The Guggenheim Museum just reopened. Tonight I
Watched a segment of the news on PBS—narrated by a
Woman we met years ago at Bob's—that showed how
Most of Wright's interior had been restored,
And how the ramp ascends in spirals towards the sky.
I like the houses better—they flow in all directions,

Merging with the scenery and embodying a milder,
More domestic notion of perfection, on a human scale
That doesn't overwhelm the life that it encloses.
Isn't there a way to feel at home within the
Confines of this bland, accommodating structure
Made of souvenirs and emblems, like the hammock
Hanging in the backyard of an undistinguished
Prairie School house in Whitefish Bay—the lineal,
Reduced descendant of the "Flameproof" Wright house
Just a block or two away from where I live now?
I usually walk along that street on Sunday,
Musing on how beautiful it seems, how aspects of it
Recapitulate the Oak Park house and studio, with
Open spaces buried in a labyrinthine interior,
And with the entrance half-concealed on the side—
A characteristic feature of his plans that made it
Difficult to find, although the hope was that in
Trying to get inside, the visitor's eye would come to
Linger over subtleties he might have failed to see—
In much the way that in the course of getting older,
And trying to reconstruct the paths that led me here,
I found myself pulled backwards through these old,
Uncertain passages, distracted by the details,
And meeting only barriers to understanding why the
Years unfolded as they did, and why my life
Turned out the way it has—like his signature
"Pathway of Discovery," with each diversion
Adding to the integrity of the whole.

There is this *sweep* life has that makes the
Accidents of time and place seem small.
Everything alters, and the personal concerns
That love could hold together for a little while
Decay, and then the world seems strange again,
And meaningless and free. I miss the primitive
Confusions, and the secret way things came to me
Each evening, and the pain. I still wonder
Where the tears went, standing in my room each day
And quietly inhabiting a calm, suspended state
Enveloped by the emptiness that scares and thrills me,
With the background noise cascading out of nothing
Like a song that makes the days go by, a song
Incorporating everything—not into what it says,
But simply in the way it touches me, a single
Image of dispersal, the inexhaustible perception
Of contingency and transience and isolation.
It brings them back to me. I have the inwardness
I think I must have wanted, and the quietude,
The solitary temper, and this space where I can
Linger with the silence curling all around me
Like the sound of pure passage, waiting here
Surrounded by the furniture, the books and lists
And all these other emblems of the floating world,
The prints of raindrops that begin as mist, that fall
Discreetly through the atmosphere, and disappear.
And then I feel them in the air, in a reserved,
More earthly music filled with voices reassembling
In a wellspring of remembrance, talking to me again,
And finding shelter in the same evasive movements

I can feel in my own life, cloaked in a quiet
Dignity that keeps away the dread of getting old,
And fading out of other people's consciousness,
And dying—with its deepest insecurities and fears
Concealed by their own protective colorations,
As the mind secretes its shell and calls it home.
It has the texture of an uncreated substance,
Hovering between the settings it had come to love
And some unformulated state I can't imagine—
Waiting for the telephone to ring, obsessed with
Ways to occupy these wide, unstructured hours,
And playing records by myself, and waking up alone.
All things are disparate, yet subject to the same
Intense, eradicating wills of time and personality,
Like waves demolishing the walls love seemed to build
Between our lives and emptiness, the certainty they
Seemed to have just two or three short years ago,
Before the anger spread its poison over everything.
I think about the way our visions locked together
In a nightmare play of nervousness and language,
Living day to day inside the concentrated
Force of that relentless argument, whose words
Swept over us in formless torrents of anxiety, two
People clinging to their versions of their lives
Almost like children—living out each other's
Intermittent fantasies, that fed upon themselves
As though infected by some vile, concentrated hatred;
Who then woke up and planned that evening's dinner.
It's all memories now, and distance. Miles away
The cat is sleeping on the driveway, John's in school,

And sunlight filters through a curtain in the kitchen.
Nothing really changes—the external world intrudes
And then withdraws, and then becomes continuous again.
I went downtown today and got a lamp with pendant
Lanterns made of opalescent art glass—part, I guess,
Of what this morning's paper called the "Wright craze."
I like the easy way the days go by, the parts of aging
That have come to seem familiar, and the uneventful
Calm that seems to settle on the house at night.
Each morning brings the mirror's reassuring face,
As though the years had left the same enduring person
Simplified and changed—no longer vaguely desperate,
No longer torn, yet still impatient with himself
And still restless; but drained of intricacy and rage,
Like a mild paradox—uninteresting in its own right,
Yet existing for the sake of something stranger.
Now and then our life comes over me, in brief,
Involuntary glimpses of that world that blossom
Unexpectedly, in fleeting moments of regret
That come before the ache, the pang that gathers
Sharply, like an indrawn breath—a strange and
Thoughtful kind of pain, as though a steel
Band had somehow snapped inside my heart.
I don't know. But what I do know is that
None of it is ever going to come to me again.
Why did I think a person only distantly like me
Might finally represent my life? What aspects
Of my attitudes, my cast of mind, my inconclusive
Way of tossing questions at the world had I
Supposed might realize another person's fantasies

And turn her into someone else—who gradually became
A separate part of me, and argued with the very
Words I would have used, and looked at me through
Eyes I'd looked at as though gazing at myself?
I guess we only realize ourselves in dreams,
Or in these self-reflexive reveries sustaining
All the charms that contemplation holds—until the
Long enchantment of the soul with what it sees
Is lifted, and it startles at a space alight with
Objects of its infantile gaze, like people in a mall.
I saw her just the other day. I felt a kind of
Comfort at her face, one tinctured with bemusement
At the strange and guarded person she'd become—
Attractive, vaguely friendly, brisk (*too* brisk),
But no one I could think might represent my life.
Why did I even *try* to see myself in what's outside?
The strangeness pushes it away, propels the vision
Back upon itself, into these regions filled with
Shapes that I can wander through and never see,
As though their image were inherently unreal.
The houses on a street, the quiet backyard shade,
The rooms restored to life with bric-a-brac—
I started by revisiting these things, then slowly
Reconceiving them as forms of loss made visible
That balanced sympathy and space inside an
Abstract edifice combining reaches of the past
With all these speculations, all this artful
Preening of the heart. I sit here at my desk,
Perplexed and puzzled, teasing out a tangled
Skein of years we wove together, and trying to

Combine the fragments of those years into a poem.
Who cares if life—if someone's actual life—is
Finally insignificant and small? There's still a
Splendor in the way it flowers once and fades
And leaves a carapace behind. There isn't time to
Linger over why it happened, or attempt to make its
Mystery come to life again and last, like someone
Still embracing the confused perceptions of himself
Embedded in the past, as though eternity lay there—
For heaven's a delusion, and eternity is in the details,
And this tiny, insubstantial life is all there is.
—And that would be enough, but for the reoccurring
Dreams I often have of you. Sometimes at night
The banished unrealities return, as though a room
Suffused with light and poetry took shape around me.
Pictures line the walls. It's early summer.
Somewhere in *Remembrance of Things Past*, Marcel,
Reflecting on his years with "Albertine"—with X—
Suggests that love is just a consciousness of distance,
Of the separation of two lives in time and space.
I think the same estrangement's mirrored in each life,
In how it seems both adequate and incomplete—part
Day-to-day existence, part imaginary construct
Beckoning at night, and sighing through my dreams
Like some disconsolate chimera, or the subject
Of a lonely, terrifying sadness; or the isolation
Of a quiet winter evening, when the house feels empty,
And silence intervenes. But in the wonderful
Enclosure opening in my heart, I seem to recognize
Our voices lilting in the yard, inflected by the

Rhythms of a song whose words are seamless
And whose lines are never-ending. I can almost
See the contours of your face, and sense the
Presence of the trees, and reimagine all of us
Together in a deep, abiding happiness, as if the
Three of us inhabited a fragile, made-up world
That seemed to be so permanent, so real.
I have this fantasy: It's early in the evening.
You and I are sitting in the backyard, talking.
Friends arrive, then drinks and dinner, conversation . . .

The lovely summer twilight lasts forever . . .

What's the use?
What purpose do these speculations serve? What
Mild enchantments do these meditations leave?
They're just the murmurs of an age, of middle age,
That help to pass the time that they retrieve
Before subsiding, leaving everything unchanged.
Each of us at times has felt the future fade,
Or seen the compass of his life diminished,
Or realized some tangible illusion was unreal.
Driving down to Evanston last week, I suddenly
Remembered driving down that road eight years ago,
So caught up in some story I'd just finished
That I'd missed the way the countryside was changing—
How in place of trees there now were office towers
And theme parks, parts of a confusing panoply of
Barns and discount malls transfiguring a landscape
Filled with high, receding clouds, and rows of flimsy

Houses in what used to be a field. I thought of
Other people's lives, and how impossible it seemed
To grasp them on the model of my own—as little
Mirrors of infinity—or sense their forms of
Happiness, or in their minor personal upheavals
Feel the sweep of time reduced to human scale
And see its abstract argument made visible.
I thought of overarching dreams of plenitude—
How life lacks shape until it's given one by love,
And how each soul is both a kingdom in itself
And part of some incorporating whole that
Feels and has a face and lets it live forever.
All of these seemed true, and cancelled one another,
Leaving just the feeling of an unseen presence
Tracing out the contours of a world erased,
Like music tracing out the contours of the mind—
For life has the form of a winding curve in space
And in its wake the human figure disappears.
Look at our surroundings—where a previous age
Could visualize a landscape we see borders,
Yet I think the underlying vision is the same:
A person positing a world that he can see
And can't contain, and vexed by other people.
Everything is possible; some of it seemed real
Or nearly real, yet in the end it spoke to me alone,
In phrases echoing the isolation of a meager
Ledge above a waterfall, or rolling across a vast,
Expanding plain on which there's always room,
But only room for one. It starts and ends
Inside an ordinary room, while in the interim

Brimming with illusions, filled with commonplace
Delights that make the days go by, with simple
Arguments and fears, and with the nervous
Inkling of some vague, utopian conceit
Transforming both the landscape and our lives,
Until we look around and find ourselves at home,
But in a wholly different world. And even those
Catastrophes that seemed to alter everything
Seem fleeting, grounded in a natural order
All of us are subject to, and ought to celebrate.
—Yet *why*? That things are temporary doesn't
Render them unreal, unworthy of regretting.
It's not as though the past had never happened:
All those years were real, and their loss was real,
And it *is* sad—I don't know what else to call it.
I'm glad that both of us seem happy. Yet what
Troubles me is just the way what used to be a world
Turned out, in retrospect, to be a state of mind,
And no more tangible than that. And now it's gone,
And in its place I find the image of a process
Of inexorable decay, or of some great unraveling
That drags the houses forward into emptiness
And backwards into pictures of the intervening days
Love pieced together out of nothing. And I'm
Certain that this austere vision finally is true,
And yet it strikes me as too meager to believe.
It comes from much too high above the world
And seems to me too hopeless, too extreme—
But then I found myself one winter afternoon
Remembering a quiet morning in a classroom

And inventing everything again, in ordinary
Terms that seemed to comprehend a childish
Dream of love, and then the loss of love,
And all the intricate years between.

Tom Bamberger

JOHN KOETHE was born in 1945 in San Diego, California, and was educated at Princeton and Harvard Universities, where he received his Ph.D. His collections of poetry include *Blue Vents* (1968), *Domes* (1973), and *The Late Wisconsin Spring* (1984). Mr. Koethe has been the recipient of the Frank O'Hara Award for Poetry, the Bernard F. Conners Award from *The Paris Review,* and Guggenheim and National Endowment for the Arts Fellowships. He is Professor of Philosophy at the University of Wisconsin–Milwaukee, and also the author of *The Continuity of Wittgenstein's Thought* (1996).